Faces, Places & Days Gone By

VOLUME 1

A Pictorial History of Michigan's Upper Peninsula

MIKEL B. CLASSEN

Modern History Press

Ann Arbor, MI

Faces, Places, and Days Gone By—Volume 1: A Pictorial History of Michigan's Upper Peninsula

Learn more at www.MikelBClassen.com
ISBN 978-1-61599-724-4 paperback
ISBN 978-1-61599-725-1 hardcover
ISBN 978-1-61599-726-8 eBook

Published by
Modern History Press   www.ModernHistoryPress.com
5145 Pontiac Trail   info@ModernHistoryPress.com
Ann Arbor, MI 48105   Tollfree 888-761-6268 (USA/CAN)
Distributed by Ingram (USA/CAN/AU).

About the cover: The cover picture is of a young girl wishing she could go for a spin on a vintage Harley Davidson. The name on the tank is clearly visible. This is from an album of vintage photos from Ishpeming, and I expect it was taken on a farm near there. This little gem is a favorite of mine. We have all had that look on our faces the moment we sat on a motorcycle.

Library of Congress Cataloging-in-Publication Data
Names: Classen, Mikel B., author.
Title: Faces, places, and days gone by : a pictorial history of Michigan's
    Upper Peninsula / Mikel B. Classen.
Other titles: Pictorial history of Michigan's Upper Peninsula
Description: Ann Arbor, MI : Modern History Press, [2023] | Includes index.
    | Contents: volume 1 : City and Settlement Life ; Homesteading ;
    Lighthouses and Lifesaving ; Logging ; Mining ; Native Americans ;
    Recreation ; Ships and Shipping ; Miscellaneous | Summary: "A broad survey of the
    history of Michigan's Upper Peninsula from mid-1800s to WW II era using postcards,
    stereoviews, lithographs, cabinet cards, and other photographic records. Each image is
    documented and sourced from a variety of topics including homesteads, lighthouses,
    timber and mining industries, Native Americans, recreation, and Great Lakes shipping
    with a focus on the Soo Locks"-- Provided by publisher.
Identifiers: LCCN 2023007018 (print) | LCCN 2023007019 (ebook) | ISBN
    9781615997244 (paperback) | ISBN 9781615997251 (hardcover) | ISBN
    9781615997268 (ebook)
Subjects: LCSH: Upper Peninsula (Mich.)--History--Pictorial works. | Upper
    Peninsula (Mich.)--History--Sources. | Classen, Mikel B.--Photograph
    collections.
Classification: LCC F572.N8 C52 2023 (print) | LCC F572.N8 (ebook) | DDC
    977.4/900222--dc23/eng/20230322
LC record available at https://lccn.loc.gov/2023007018
LC ebook record available at https://lccn.loc.gov/2023007019

Contents

Dedication

For all of those photographer explorers who risked life and limb to document the Faces, Places and Days Gone By for history. Without these intrepid explorers, capturers of the windows of the past, we would only be able to imagine from historical writings. Due to their great determination and tenacity, we can look back across the years and truly see the days of the lives of those that made the Upper Peninsula what it is today.

Introduction—The Mikel B. Classen Historical Pictures Collection

As a historian, I have a good grasp of what life in the past must have looked like, but there is nothing like having photographs to accurately see our world in the early days of the evolution of our society. Very rarely do we look at ourselves as historical, but as time passes and events occur, the ripples from those days gone by leave their marks on individuals and communities. We go about our lives and routines, unaware that our passing through time will leave indelible marks on history.

The invention of photography gave the world momentary windows of time preserved for the future to see. Photographs help us accurately depict and learn about life as we all move through time. Even though we don't think about it now, someday someone will be looking back at all the Instagram and FaceBook pictures to try to explain life in the 2000s. All I have to say is, good luck with that.

The Mikel B. Classen Historical Pictures Collection began as an effort to facilitate my research and be able to accurately peer into the past for accuracy. It didn't take long for it to evolve into much more than that. I soon found images from across the Upper Peninsula, which sent me on their own investigations spurred by the curiosity behind the photos. The pictures took many forms, from old engravings and lithographs, to rare stereoviews, postcards, cabinet cards, and press release photos. You can learn more about the types of images used here by flipping right to the Glossary in the back of this book.

There are currently around 1000 images in the collection with more being added all of the time. This book contains over 100 of the pictures, displaying a cross-section of time and life in Michigan's Upper Peninsula. I tried to pick a diversity of locations and subjects that would interest and fascinate any lover of the U.P. Now I get to share them with others.

When looking through the pictures in this book, consider that a photographer is involved in each image. Each picture was taken by someone who often went to extreme lengths to get the pictures. They would have to pack heavy and awkward equipment, often to remote or even dangerous locations just to get the pictures we see. They would have portable wagons that carried picture plates and developing chemicals. The photographers could develop pictures on the spot. They were dedicated daredevils who would do almost anything for the perfect picture. The older the picture, the heavier and more cumbersome the equipment was. They themselves were rugged pioneers and explorers who were unsung through history.

I feel lucky and privileged to be the caretaker of these historical artifacts. Preserving the past for the future is an important task, and when I get new additions to the collection, I feel it is something coming back home where it belongs, where it will enhance our knowledge and education, will be cherished and used to further the pursuit of history, U.P. history.

With this book, it is my hope that these images will now have an opportunity to be enjoyed by others instead of languishing in my drawers and on my shelves. I enjoy looking at them and I hope others will as well. I've written concise summaries of each one with as much information as is available. These discuss the details and nuances of what we can learn from the individual image. Enjoy these gems from the Mikel B. Classen Historical Pictures collection.

Mikel B. Classen
2023

Introduction—The Mikel B. Classen Historical Pictures Collection

As a historian, I have a good grasp of what life in the past must have looked like, but there is nothing like having photographs to accurately see our world in the early days of the evolution of our society. Very rarely do we look at ourselves as historical, but as time passes and events occur, the ripples from those days gone by leave their marks on individuals and communities. We go about our lives and routines, unaware that our passing through time will leave indelible marks on history.

The invention of photography gave the world momentary windows of time preserved for the future to see. Photographs help us accurately depict and learn about life as we all move through time. Even though we don't think about it now, someday someone will be looking back at all the Instagram and FaceBook pictures to try to explain life in the 2000s. All I have to say is, good luck with that.

The Mikel B. Classen Historical Pictures Collection began as an effort to facilitate my research and be able to accurately peer into the past for accuracy. It didn't take long for it to evolve into much more than that. I soon found images from across the Upper Peninsula, which sent me on their own investigations spurred by the curiosity behind the photos. The pictures took many forms, from old engravings and lithographs, to rare stereoviews, postcards, cabinet cards, and press release photos. You can learn more about the types of images used here by flipping right to the Glossary in the back of this book.

There are currently around 1000 images in the collection with more being added all of the time. This book contains over 100 of the pictures, displaying a cross-section of time and life in Michigan's Upper Peninsula. I tried to pick a diversity of locations and subjects that would interest and fascinate any lover of the U.P. Now I get to share them with others.

When looking through the pictures in this book, consider that a photographer is involved in each image. Each picture was taken by someone who often went to extreme lengths to get the pictures. They would have to pack heavy and awkward equipment, often to remote or even dangerous locations just to get the pictures we see. They would have portable wagons that carried picture plates and developing chemicals. The photographers could develop pictures on the spot. They were dedicated daredevils who would do almost anything for the perfect picture. The older the picture, the heavier and more cumbersome the equipment was. They themselves were rugged pioneers and explorers who were unsung through history.

I feel lucky and privileged to be the caretaker of these historical artifacts. Preserving the past for the future is an important task, and when I get new additions to the collection, I feel it is something coming back home where it belongs, where it will enhance our knowledge and education, will be cherished and used to further the pursuit of history, U.P. history.

　　With this book, it is my hope that these images will now have an opportunity to be enjoyed by others instead of languishing in my drawers and on my shelves. I enjoy looking at them and I hope others will as well. I've written concise summaries of each one with as much information as is available. These discuss the details and nuances of what we can learn from the individual image. Enjoy these gems from the Mikel B. Classen Historical Pictures collection.

Mikel B. Classen
2023

City and Settlement Life

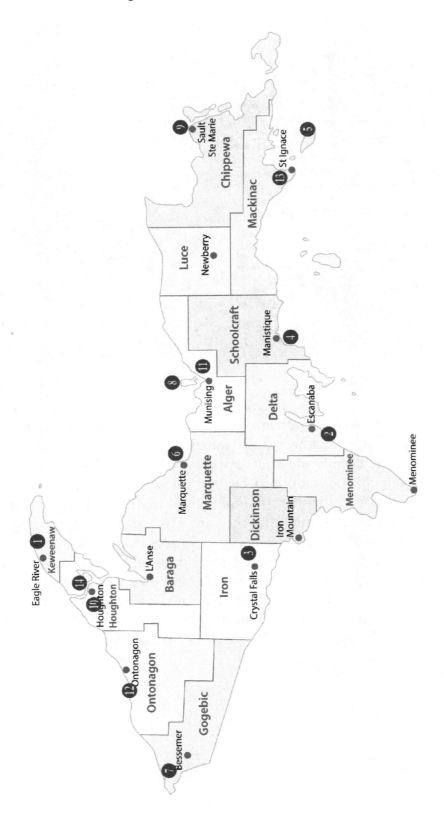

❶ Cliff Mine Settlement—Keweenaw Peninsula

Deserted Village, Old Cliff Mine, Calumet, Mich.

Photography by Tom Jones

Postcard

The Cliff Mine settlement was one of the earliest in the Upper Peninsula. Established in 1845, it ranks as the first ore producing copper mine in the Keweenaw that was an organized company. Copper had been dug by ancient pit miners (Native Americans) all across the region. An old legend states that copper was discovered here when a prospector or trapper fell down a cliff face and hurt his butt on a projecting piece of copper. The picture, a vintage postcard, shows the community that sprang up around the mine and is taken around the turn of the century after the Cliff Mine was shut down and the village abandoned. From 1845–1854, it was the most productive copper mine in the U.S., producing over $2.5 million worth of ore. That is the equivalent of $56 million today. Silver was also produced. The mine's heyday was over by 1878, and mining was through by 1887. The date on the postcard is 1906, and it contains a message: "You are a dandy chaperone. We enjoyed your company so much at the party." It is addressed to Mr. M.J. Smith, Eagle Harbor, Michigan, who is apparently a dandy chaperone.

❷ Dog Sled Race in the Streets—Escanaba

Photography by Unknown   *Photograph*

Winter along the Great Lakes can be long and hard. Much of life was spent simply trying to stay warm. Occasionally though, the weather breaks and some fun begins. Dog sleds were common in the early days of the Upper Peninsula. They were a tool for mobility in winter as much as the horse was. The racers have found a good day for some fun and it looks like much of the town has turned out to watch the competition. One of the things to notice is the wooden store fronts. Though there is no date on the picture, it seems to be late 1800s. Driving around Escanaba, a few of these types of buildings can still be seen. Though Escanaba claims 1863 as its founding date, its name came from a Anishinaabe word that identified a native village already established there.

❸ Future Metropolis of the U.P.—Iron River

Photography by E. Ammermann   *Postcard*

There is no shortage of high hopes in this one. This "bird's eye" view is from a postcard promoting Iron River as a booming community. Like many towns on the iron range, Iron River was actively seeking residents to work in the mines that were springing up everywhere in that part of the peninsula. Iron County, where Iron River is located, had over 50 iron mines. One of the takeaways from the picture is the lack of trees. In places, the ground is completely bare. Logging was the other big local industry. The hills and forests surrounding the community were full of loggers and the results of their work is clearly evident. Iron River had about 5,000 residents at its peak, certainly not quite a metropolis, but unlike many of the cities in the region, the population has remained reasonably steady. To this day, Iron River is a thriving community that is a paradise for outdoor recreation.

④ Motorcycle Hitting the Streets—Manistique

Photograph by E.O Brault   *Postcard*

This picture is probably from the early 1920s. Even back in the old days, there was nothing like a cruise on the bike. The biker, dressed in the finest of early riding gear, is showing his ride off down main street Manistique. At this time, he could easily have had the only motorcycle in town. In the picture, all eyes are on him. The dog is looking at him, the child is looking at him and the pedestrian is looking at him. To the dog's credit, he doesn't seem inclined to chase the bike. Good dog. Look closely and there is a bunch of guys looking out the window, trying to get a look at the motorcycle. The sign overhead says "Bowling," so it is probably a saloon. There are at least four if not five viewers from there. The picture reinforces the idea that seeing the motorcycle was not common at the time. The photographer probably knew the biker and set this scene up.

❺ Enjoying the View from the Overlook—Mackinac Island

Photograph by P.B. Greene   *Cabinet Card*

This provides a wonderful view of the harbor and village at Mackinac Island. It seems to be taken from near Fort Mackinac at the top of the hill. The couple are enjoying the view, wearing wonderful period clothing. They also seem cold as they are both wrapped in blankets around their legs. This picture was shot sometime around 1880. It is part of a series of pictures titled "Views of the National Park." In 1875, Mackinac Island became the second national park after Yellowstone. The island was a huge attraction and dozens of cruise ships made it a regular stop. In 1895, the Federal government gave up Mackinac Island and returned it to the State of Michigan. It was then turned into Michigan's first state park. To this day, Mackinac Island usually turns up on everyone's travel list at some time or another.

6   **J.W. Spear Rolling Mill Store—Marquette**

Photograph by Unknown   *Cabinet Card*

This picture came to me as part of a larger collection. It features the J. W. Spear Rolling Mill Store. For many years the Spear family owned several businesses, including a large lumber mill. They maintained a large warehouse at the Lower Harbor in Marquette for a long time, but condos now occupy its location. The picture shows several folks who either work at the store or are customers. Maybe both. However, the buckboard wagon really makes this picture a prize. The muddy road and wooden sidewalk are like something out of an old movie, not to mention the classic building.

7 **Ironwood Bad Boys—Ironwood**

Photograph by O.L. Thornbladh   *Cabinet Card*

This is a favorite picture of mine. The names of the men above are unknown, but they're surely trouble waiting for a place to happen. All of these guys look like they are someone you wouldn't want to mess with. Their faces seem to have that "we mean business" look, though we will never know what business they mean. I get the feeling that the two guys with the bowler hats are under arrest and the three standing behind them are the sheriff and deputies. I have seen other pictures similar to this that show this very same pose for captured crooks near Ironwood. This photo is from the rough and tumble days of the U.P. and they look like they could have personally provided some of that rough and tumble.

8 **Williams Landing—Grand Island**

Photography by Ferguson   *Postcard*

"Williams Landing" is one of the oldest place names on Lake Superior. In the early days, it was a way-station for voyageurs and a staging area for exploring Pictured Rocks. It became an early resort area that attracted visitors from all over. It was in public hands, and remains so to this day. The name comes from Abraham Williams, who moved there in 1850 with his family and established a trading post. They were among some of the earliest settlers on the Lake Superior frontier. The picture dates from the early 1900s and shows some of the original homesteads along with the Williams' house. The Williams family is still buried on the island in one of the oldest cemeteries of Europeans in the Upper Peninsula. They shared the island with a small band of Ojibwa Native Americans. A picture of their settlement is later in the book. The postmark is 1913.

❾ Hotel Iroquois—Sault Ste. Marie

Photography by Rosin & Co.   *Postcard)*

The Hotel Iroquois was located on Portage Street in Sault Ste. Marie. Situated across from the Soo Locks, it was the elite place to stay in the city. The beautiful architecture made it stand apart from everything around it, and the interior was immaculate. It was built during an age when places to stay boasted grand porches and service fit for royalty. A need for this kind of lodging was perceived by a William Smith of Cheboygan, who dismantled the Mullet Lake Househotel piece-by-piece and sent it on a ship to the Sault in 1886. He then had it reconstructed across from where the Locks visitor center sits now. It opened in 1887 and was a Victorian palace. It burned down after 10 years and a second Hotel Iroquois was built on the ashes of the old. The picture above is of the second version. It stood for 10 years as well, and then suffered the fate of the first and burned down in 1907. The card is dated Aug 1, 1912, which would be after the first hotel had burned down. A small message on the card says, "Have had a fine trip—Lake is grand, Lill."

⑩   Billiard Room and Parlor—South Range

Photography by Unknown   *Cabinet Card*

Billiards anyone? This is a rare shot inside a billiard room and parlor, which were very popular throughout the Upper Peninsula. Every town had at least one. This one appears to also have a munchie case for food.   Pool is a game that has never dwindled in popularity and this seems to be no exception. The two tables are full and the two reading a paper and sitting are probably waiting for their turn for a round. This picture is a nice look into daily life and shows how to kill a few hours.

⑪   Early Munising—Munising

Photography by Unknown   *Stereoview*

Munising was established in the 1870s, noted at the time for the pig iron furnaces that were built there. Surrounded by logging, the region thrived and grew quickly. The picture above is from the early days of Munising, and the lack of trees is evident. Stumps can be seen in the background on the hill. Taken in 1892 and labeled "Old Munising," the town was a fledgling community and would eventually grow to the beautiful city we know today. The word Munising is taken from an Ojibwa word meaning "near the island," referring to Grand Island, which sits in Munising Bay. Eventually the natural harbor at Munising made it a harbor of refuge crucial to the survival of ships on Lake Superior. The abundance of hardwoods and pines supplied the Munising Wooden Ware Company, the producer of the legendary Munising woodenware.

⑫ New Homes of Victoria—Rockland

Photograph by Ferguson   *Postcard*

Victoria was a town that grew around the Victoria Copper Mine and the Forest Mining Company near Rockland along the Ontonagon River. It was not far from where the legendary Ontonagon Boulder sat. Alexander Henry, the British explorer, tried to mine copper near the Victoria location, which became the first European mining venture. The Forest Mining Company moved there in the late 1890s. They began digging the Victoria Mine, and a small community of miners and their families sprung up around it, including a substantial Finnish population. The picture above shows the fresh-built houses, some of which still stand. The mine closed in 1921, and the settlement was abandoned. Old Victoria, as it is now called, stands as one of the premier ghost towns in the U.P. Much of it has achieved restoration and is a part of the Keweenaw National Historical Park. The postcard is postmarked 1914. The message is entirely in Finnish.

⓭ St. Ignace with Mackinac Island—St. Ignace

Copyright 1913, By G. H. Wickman. Made in Germany.   St. Ignace, Mich., Showing Mackinac Island in the Distance.

Photography by G. H. Wickman   *Cabinet Card*

St. Ignace is one of the oldest cities in Michigan. Founded in 1670 by the Jesuit explorer, Jacques Marquette, the city is steeped in history. It has a close association with Mackinac Island and its colonial past. St. Ignace had a French fort, Fort De Baude, that was garrisoned for many years, but its actual location seems lost to time. The picture above shows Mackinac Island, St. Ignace harbor in Lake Huron, and St. Ignace itself. The photo is dated 1913. Looking closely, we can see several kinds of ships in the harbor: a schooner, a steamer, and a car ferry are clear. Many of the buildings in this picture still stand, and St. Ignace is a tourist destination that retains much of its antiquity.

14 Quincy Street—Hancock

Photograph by Hugh C. Leighton   *Postcard*

Quincy Street in Hancock was a bustling place during the heyday of the Copper Boom. The building on the right is the Northern Michigan Building and Loan Association. Look very carefully down the street to see furs hanging over the sidewalk, and a pack mule standing in the street. It says a lot about life in the Copper Country at the time. Electric wires crisscross the skyline and strings of light bulbs hang overhead. The street is still dirt—wheel ruts can be plainly seen. Hancock is Houghton's twin, separated by the Portage Canal. Many of Hancock's old buildings still stand, echoing the prosperous past. It was a city steeped in the riches of copper.

Homesteading

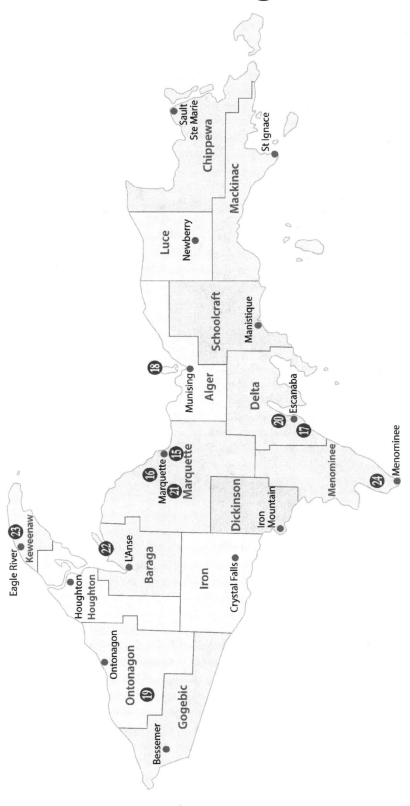

⑮   On the Homestead—Marquette

Photograph by C. B. Brubaker   *Stereoview*

A log cabin like this homestead somewhere near Marquette would have been tough to build. The logs must have been heavy to get that high in the air. The wash is hung out on the line. The photograph is a typical picture of settlers trying to bust open a piece of land from the dense wilderness. Much of the Upper Peninsula soil was poor for growing, so establishing a garden was difficult at best. Hunting was good, as was foraging for berries. Fish abounded in the lakes and streams. Chores to get through tomorrow took all day. It was wet, muddy and buggy. There are hardly any windows in the cabin making, it dark, and escape would be difficult if it caught on fire. These people came to carve out a life, and they succeeded no matter what it took.

⑯ Group Photo on a Fence—Ishpeming

Photograph by N. M. Nelson   *Cabinet Card*

Rural life in the early days of the U.P. was rough, but of course folks found a way to make the best of it. This group dressed up for the photographer and lined up along a split rail fence. Getting a photo taken back then was a big deal. Arrangements were made, everyone dressed in their proverbial Sunday best. The homestead can be seen in the background. There is no information on the card, except "Farm near Ishpeming." The individuals in the picture are unknown though they all seem to be having a very fine day.

⑰ The Sunday Buggy Ride—Powers

Photograph by Unknown   *Postcard*

This is a personalized early postcard showing people going to church on Sunday. Occasionally, a person could get their own pictures printed as postcards or even stereoviews. This one is from Powers near Escanaba and is dated 1909. Dressed up for Sunday, the horse harnessed for the trip, this couple is ready to roll. The weekly trips to church often culminated in a community picnic or gathering, a weekly social event. People talked about their lives and knew one another intimately. If a person missed a Sunday, everyone would know and worry something had befallen them and look in on them. It gave meaning to the words "neighborly," and "community."

⑱ Grand Island Settler—Munising

OLD SETTLER GRAND ISLAND, NEAR MUNISING, MICHIGAN.

Photograph by Unknown *Postcard*

It took sturdy individuals to settle the harshness of the U.P. wilderness. The person in this picture is certainly one of those. Grand Island is in Lake Superior. Thanks to the Williams family, a trading post thrived here, doing a good business in fur trading. I believe the building in the picture still stands. It is labeled as a fur storage warehouse. It was the fur trade that led to the settlements of the early years. The card is labeled "Old Settler Grand Island." Unfortunately he is not identified. There is also no date for this and there aren't enough details to put a date on it. The face on this old settler shows the harsh weathering of a life on Lake Superior.

19 **Unknown Family—Rockland**

Photograph by W. M. Horton   *Cabinet Card*

Rockland is a town southeast of Ontonagon. The terrain is rugged, and several copper mines were nearby. The village is remote even by today's standards. Records of Rockland begin in 1847 with the opening of the Minnesota Mine. The small town was carved out of the surrounding mountainous hills that had been created by the glaciers and the Ontonagon River. The picture above shows an early Rockland family. These faces could be seen in the community. Though the picture is unidentified, these are the people who had lived there. These types of portraits show us who was walking down the streets of the past. It also shows how they looked at the time. The picture is from the 1880s and the clothing reflects the period. The hat the woman on the right is holding is classic. It would have been cool if she had worn it.

㉕ Supply Wagons—Escanaba

Photograph by Unknown   *Postcard*

Getting supplies delivered across the U.P. was problematic. The dense wilderness made roadways or trails few, and those that existed were rough. Given the long winters, if supplies didn't arrive, it was quickly a life and death situation. Some areas were serviced by ships while others were fortunate enough to have access to the railroad, but homesteads and many of the small isolated towns had to depend on wagon shipments like the one pictured. This was taken from a postcard dated 1915. The message on the card says, "Kind sir, would you please be kind enough to send me my rig at Escanaba." A rig at the time referred to a wagon and harness set. It was necessary equipment for survival.

㉑   Wash Day—Ishpeming

Photograph by Unknown   *Photo Print*

No washers, no dryers, no laundromats. This is how it used to be done. Take a little soap that had to be made at home, too, a washboard, and a lot of arm work. Scrubbing laundry on a washboard was intense labor. In the picture, there is a kid leaning out the window, watching the older women do the hard work. After rinsing, the clothes had to be run through a wringer to squeeze out the excess water before the clothes were then hung out on a clothesline. There is a reason no one pursues this method today. It is backbreaking work and incredibly hard on the hands, especially the knuckles, which are constantly scraped on the washboard.

㉒ Depths of the Wilderness—Huron Bay

Photograph by Unknown   *Stereoview*

The denseness of the U.P. before logging is hard to picture. Though the regrowth of time has allowed much of it to come back, the difficulties of simply carving out a foothold, let alone a homestead with a cabin, cannot be overstated. This stereoview shows how hard it was to make a place for a tent within the thick forest. The stovepipe sticking out of the tent door shows how they battled the cold of the Lake Superior weather. This was not a lifestyle for the faint of heart. This picture is from 1860 or earlier. The man in front is leaning on his rifle and his beard goes to his waist. This is an amazing image from the earliest days of the settlement of the U.P.

㉓ Fort Wilkins Before Restoration—Copper Harbor

Fort Wilkins, Keweenaw, Mich. 58.

Photograph by Unknown   *Postcard*

Fort Wilkins is currently one of the most popular state parks in Michigan. Its place in history is undisputed in providing a foothold for the early copper rush. It was established in 1844 as an army outpost. Named after the Secretary of War at the time, William Wilkins, the post was to help keep law and order at the time as large deposits of copper were being discovered. Some of the local Ojibwa were unwilling to accept the Treaty of La Pointe, which had ceded the land to the U.S. government, opening it up for homesteading miners. Trouble was anticipated and the army was garrisoned at Fort Wilkins. No trouble ever arose, and within a few years the troops were withdrawn and Fort Wilkins became obsolete. The picture shows the fort before it was restored by the State of Michigan. After the fort was decommissioned, it was turned into a health resort for those needing cooler climate therapy. That lasted a little over a decade.

24   On the Haystack—Menominee

Photograph by Unknown   *Photo Print*

Growing up on the homestead often meant finding your fun where you could. Before TV, before the internet, there was jumping into the haystack. Entertaining oneself back then often required some thought and a lot of invention. The picture, from the 1920s, has two girls in period clothing posing on a haystack for whoever had the camera. The old man probably would like to get on with his work of putting the hay into the barn. Life in those days was exactly what you made it.

㉕ Gaining a Foothold—Isle Royale

Photograph by Unknown   *Cabinet Card*

This is an early picture, labeled Isle Royale. Gaining a foothold on the island with the building and a dock was the beginning of a settlement. The group of people can be seen sitting on freshly lumbered boards. Parts of a schooner, the mast and the stern, show from behind the building. This is probably Rock Harbor, but there is no designation on the picture. A close look at the people in the picture reveals the faces and the fashions of 1870. This is a truly rare photograph.

Lighthouses and Lifesaving

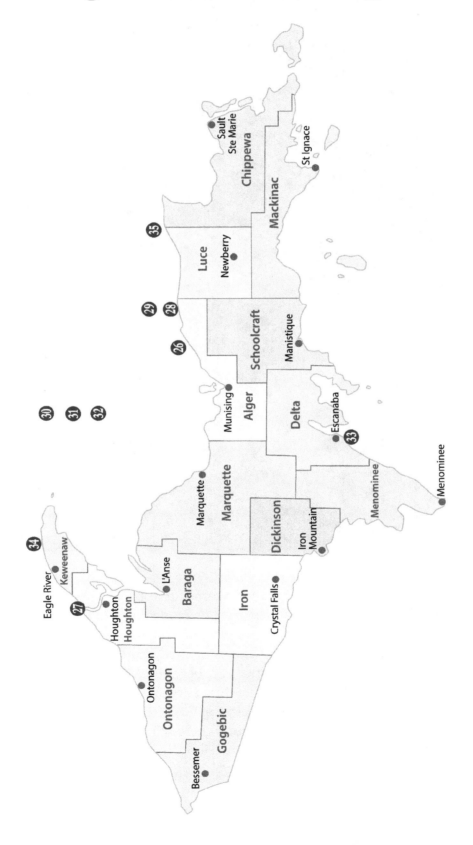

26 Death on Lake Superior—Pictured Rocks

Image by Thomas Moran   *Lithograph*

This is an early drawing by artist Thomas Moran. It aptly depicts the dangers of sailing the Great Lakes in the early days. Immediately recognizable is Chapel Rock from Pictured Rocks. A thunderstorm rages, and a man drowns in the foreground. His sinking ship can be seen on the horizon. When the Soo Locks opened, shipping greatly increased across Lake Superior. So did shipwrecks. In one year, between Marquette and Whitefish Point, 212 men were lost to Superior's tantrums. In a very short span of time, lighthouses and lifesaving stations were erected throughout the Great Lakes. They saved countless lives and prevented dozens of shipwrecks. Though there would still be shipwrecks and loss of life, pursuing the life of a mariner was greatly improved.

㉗ **Portage Entry Lighthouse—Houghton**

Photograph by C. Kropp Co.   *Postcard*

This was a very important lighthouse. It marked the entry to the Portage Canal, which gave lake access to Houghton, Hancock, Lake Linden, and Dollar Bay. Constructed in 1868, it not only showed the way to the rapidly growing cities of the Keweenaw, but also improved the safety of the Portage Canal when Lake Superior was violent. A breakwater was built and another light was placed on the end of the pier, which allowed navigators to line the lights up to get an exact position. These were also known as range lights. The lightkeepers kept these lights burning nightly through the shipping season. They were a dedicated lot who were often stationed with their families. There are instances where the keeper died and his wife took over with the same diligence as the husband. This lighthouse no longer exists, and there is a park where it once stood. Modern lights on the breakwater now perform the same function.

㉘ Life Saving Station Extraordinaire—Grand Marais

Photograph by Unknown   *Postcard*

Located at the heart of the Lake Superior Shipwreck Coast, this particular life saving station saw more than its share of action. Shipwrecks here were frequent because of a sandstone reef that caught more ships than most places, so a life saving station here, 8 miles east of Au Sable Point, was essential. Life saving stations were different from lighthouses, though most life saving stations also had a light. They were manned by a specially trained crew that would row out into the teeth of the worst storm to save passengers and crews of ships in distress. One of the most noted at this was the life savers at Grand Marais. They became the standard for life savers within the service. The life saving service would eventually be rolled into today's Coast Guard. It cannot be overstated how vital and important the service was to travel on the Great Lakes.

㉙ Life Savers in Action—Grand Marais

Capt. Trudell and his Gallant Crew going to relief of ship in distress,
Grand Marais, Michigan.

Photograph by J. Verne Kinsey   *Postcard*

The life saver crew in action is pictured above. The crew practiced every day when there wasn't a shipwreck. The image shows Captain Trudell, the commander of the Grand Marais lifesaving station, and his well-trained crew. Their determination in the face of Lake Superior's worst storms made them legendary within the service. The picture shows what all of the life saving crews went through all around the Great Lakes. They trained, and trained, and then trained some more. They sprang into action when a ship was in distress. They lived up to their own mantra, "The service says we have to go out, it doesn't say we have to come back." And in some cases, they didn't come back, having sacrificed their lives to give others a chance to live.

㉚ Remote and Rugged Lighthouse—Isle Royale

THE RUGGED SHORE AND LIGHTHOUSE, ISLE ROYALE, LAKE SUPERIOR—3

Photograph by E. C. Kropp   *Postcard*

Many lighthouses were placed in remote and uninhabited places. When a lightkeeper was dropped there in the spring, their only other contact was a supply boat. The lightkeepers were allowed to have their families with them, but this was a hard lifestyle for anyone. The light had to be maintained every day along with upkeep on the building. With little or no contact, some of the keepers went a little crazy from isolation, and had to be reassigned to some other duty. Islands like Isle Royale were the hardest. Often, they were little more than large rock outcrops that were hazards to navigation. Life was not easy, but in these places it was even harder. Unbridled weather, with no communications, made surviving difficult. Yet, the dedication of the lightkeepers kept the lights burning. Every self-respecting lighthouse has a ghost still trying to keep the light burning.

㉛ Impending Doom—Lake Superior

Photograph by Unknown   *Postcard*

When they are in the mood, the Great Lakes can turn ships into playthings, destroying them in the matter of a moment. The story has been repeated often: lost without a trace, presumed dead. The monster waves that can be generated, especially on Lake Superior, can dwarf the largest freighters. The picture above shows a ship in major distress as the waves batter the hull. It would be in these kinds of swells that the life savers were called out. As soon as the cold water came in contact with the steam boiler in the back, a horrific explosion occurred, which tore the rear of the ship apart. The life savers searched for survivors and maybe found a few, but the remains of the freighter and those who didn't make it remained entombed on the lake bottom.

㉜ Disaster Strikes—Lake Superior

Photograph by United Press Association   *Press Release Photo*

All too often men die due to the Great Lakes. The picture above is a press release photo. I like them as they depict history, but the images are usually labeled and captioned. The information on them is fairly complete. The back of this one states: "A lifeboat carrying two crewmen of the freighter *Henry Steinbrenner* which sank in Lake Superior, May 11th, is reached by the rescue ship William Sykes. The man at bottom of lifeboat, identified as Frank Tomszak, was dead when reached by rescuers. Other crewman rescued here was identified as Bernard Oberski." The *Henry Steinbrenner* was caught in a storm and the hatches began taking on water. The crew was eventually ordered to abandon ship and several survivors were picked up. Ships in the area searched for lifeboats, but 17 men were lost total. It was 1953, the Life Saving Service had been rolled in the U.S. Coast Guard and the role of life savers fell to those in the area.

㉝ Sand Point Lighthouse—Escanaba

Photograph by Unknown   *Postcard*

The Sand Point Lighthouse has shown since 1868 and it was lit by a woman. It warned mariners of a sandbar that was at the entrance to Escanaba Harbor. Construction began on Sand Point in 1864 and the first lightkeeper was named John Terry. He oversaw the construction and prepared the lighthouse for occupation along with his wife, Mary. Just before the light was supposed to be lit, John Terry died. Sand Point was scheduled to begin its beacon on May 13, 1868. Mary Terry made sure that happened and took over from her husband. She was officially appointed lightkeeper, making her one of the very first women lightkeepers on the Great Lakes. She served until 1888 when she was killed in a freak fire in the lighthouse. She was one of several women who faithfully served in the Lighthouse Service.

34 Wreck of the City of Bangor—Copper Harbor

Photograph by Unknown   *Postcard*

The gales of November in this case turned to snow and ice. On November 30, 1926 the ship, *City of Bangor*, ran onto the shore of the Keweenaw. Nearly encased in ice, the ship was carrying over 250 Chryslers. Some can be seen in the picture as square blocks of ice on the deck. Many of them broke loose during the storm and went overboard. The crew broke the lifeboats loose and made it to shore. They then began to walk back to Copper Harbor and became lost. They built a fire and struggled through the freezing night. The next day, the Life Saving Service out of Eagle Harbor found them while rescuing the crew of another ship that had run aground at the same time. They took one crew and came back for the crew of the City of Bangor. In the hold of the City of Bangor, there sat over 200 new Chryslers, dry in a still secure hold. It was decided to rescue them. An ice bridge with a ramp was built to the ship and the Chryslers were driven off. It had been cold enough that an ice shelf had developed and it was decided to drive the cars on the Lake Superior ice to Copper Harbor. The rescue was a success for men and cars.

35 **Vermillion Life Saving Station—Whitefish Point**

33. Vermilion Point Life Saving Station, one of five between Grand Marais and White Fish Point, on Lake Superior.

Copyright '07 by J. V. Kinsey, Grand Marais, Mich. – Made in Germany

Photograph by J.V. Kinsey   *Postcard*

The Vermillion Life Saving Station was a part of a string of Life Saving Stations that were from Whitefish Point to Grand Marais. Established in 1877, it was part of a group of stations along the famed Lake Superior Shipwreck Coast that included Grand Marais, Deer Park, Big Two-Hearted River, Crisp Point and Vermillion. They were situated about 20 miles apart and watched over the entire section of Lake Superior. Out of all of these stations only Grand Marais and Vermillion have buildings from the life saving service still standing. The light tower is all that is left at Crisp Point.

Logging

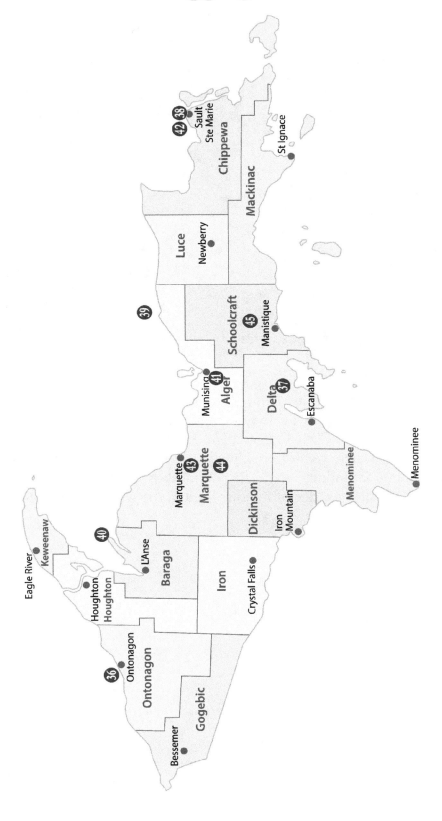

36 Logging Crew at Camp—Ontonagon

Photograph by Unknown   *Postcard*

This is a rare picture of a lumber camp near Ontonagon. It is the beginning of the season and the men are preparing for the long winter ahead. A message on the back of this card gives insight into that life. "Hello Erma, Here is the real thing. Now I am 14 miles from town and I can't get there very often. I have to go out the first of October and I will send you something and Grandma too." The postmark is 1911. Lumber camps dotted every part of the U.P. and thousands of men worked in the woods every winter.

③⑦ Loggers in the Woods—Rapid River

Photograph by Unknown   *Post Card*

This crew of loggers was working on the woods near Rapid River. Horse teams were essential to logging the Upper Peninsula. During winter, horses would skid the logs across the snow to where they could be loaded onto a logging cart. There is no date on this, but from the clothes I place it in the 1920-30s range. These guys look as if they had a long day before the photographer got there. Even the horses look ready for a break. This was incredibly hard and dangerous work. Loggers were a tough bunch, but they had to be to battle the brutal cold while working dawn until dusk.

38 **Log Raft in the Soo Locks—Sault Ste. Marie**

Photograph by L. L. Cook   *Postcard*

This is a picture of the Soo Locks around 1930. It shows logging practices during a peak period in history. An immense log raft is shown inside the locks, necessary to get the logs from the shoreline to the sawmills. A chain of logs encompassed free-floating logs towed across the water by a ship or tug. This was a long way from being a foolproof plan and many logs were lost in the unpredictable waters or the Great Lakes.

㊴ Logs to Be Rafted at Hurricane Creek—Grand Marais

12   On Lake Superior at mouth of Hurricane Creek showing logs to be rafted,
near Grand Marais, Mich.

Photograph by J. V. Kinsey   *Postcard*

Logging on the Lake Superior shoreline was a difficult process at best, but despite this, the forests were cut in a remarkably short amount of time. The picture shows the beginnings of a mountain of logs, soon to be floated to the Sault in log chain rafts. The logs were cut and stacked in the winter and then floated away during the fairer weather. The man in the boat is not paying any attention to the logs, but looking at the shipwreck of the *Mary Jarecki*, which can be plainly seen in the foreground. Stacks of logs like this dotted the shoreline at staging areas across the Great Lakes.

40 Logging Camp and Sawmill—Skanee

Photograph by Unknown   *Cabinet Card*

Logging camps and sawmills were located everywhere across the Upper Peninsula. This one was in Skanee, and was a thriving camp at one point. Skanee was extremely remote with access only by ship for many years. Located on Lake Superior's Huron Bay, this would have been a hard life. The picture was in rough shape when I got it. Details aren't the best, but one thing that can be seen is the size of the trees waiting to be milled. The forests of the U.P. provided well for the loggers and the world at large.

41 **Immense Wagon of Logs—Munising**

Photograph by Unknown   *Postcard*

Occasionally, there turns up a picture showing massive loads of logs on a sledge. These loads were pulled by horses and mules. I've seen pictures like this accused of being faked or photoshopped. They are quite real. Loggers were paid by the number of trees they cut down, including a bonus for oversized trees. A logger could have a tree with enough girth that it would count for two or three trees by only cutting one. This is one of the reasons many of our largest trees no longer exist. Also, the White Pine was extremely popular for home building and the reconstruction of Chicago after the Great Fire.

42 Lumber Tow Leaving the Soo—Sault Ste. Marie

Lumber Tow leaving Soo, Mich.

Photograph by Young, Lord & Rhodes   *Postcard*

When the lumber had been milled, the finished wood was loaded aboard ships and then transported to Chicago or Detroit, where it was sold on the market. The decks and holds of the ships were loaded, in many cases overloaded, with boards or sheets of veneer. The image above shows a tow of ships, something that was common on the Great Lakes. One main ship towed several others with a long rope. The following ships only had a few men as crew, nowhere near a full complement. This occasionally led to disaster when the weather turned bad. With a skeleton crew, held together by a single rope line, these groups of ships would shipwreck all at once, often killing everyone involved.

43 **Negaunee Sawmill—Negaunee**

Photograph by A. G. Busselman   *Postcard*

This is a nice group shot of a sawmill in Negaunee, showing the number of men it took to run that kind of operation. The postmark is 1903. There are close to fifty men working in this one mill, showing that these were not easily run. The photographer had to have spent quite a bit of time getting all of these guys together and setting this up to show the mill at its peak. Manpower in those days was the key to success and these are the hands who tamed the Upper Peninsula wilderness.

44 Logging the Woods—Trenary

Photograph by Unknown   *Postcard*

Early on, the loggers took both pines and hardwoods. The old growth forests provided plenty of both. The picture shows how much of the area had been cut out, and the scarcity of the remaining trees. In many pictures from across the U.P., the lack of trees after logging is hard to believe. It shows how resilient the forests are. Travelling through the dense forests of the Upper Peninsula, keep in mind that at one time nearly every acre has been logged at least once. Much of the U.P. has returned to the Midwest rainforest that it once was. Though logging continues to this day, conservation methods continuously monitor the health of our forests.

45 Logging Crew at Camp—Manistique

Photograph by Alfred Cook   *Postcard*

This is a small crew at a logging camp. Located somewhere near Manistique, this rough cut old camp must have been warm and cozy. The roof has been shoveled to keep the snow from piling up. There is a grinding wheel for axes sitting in front of the guy on the left. There are no names to identify the individuals, but they look like hardy souls. On the right is a boy who probably keeps the fires going while the others are out harvesting logs. Small crews like this were not unusual and the men had to know each other well to be able to work together and trust each other, as logging was extremely dangerous. If a tree kicked out or fell the wrong way, trying to get out of the way in deep snow could be fatal.

Mining

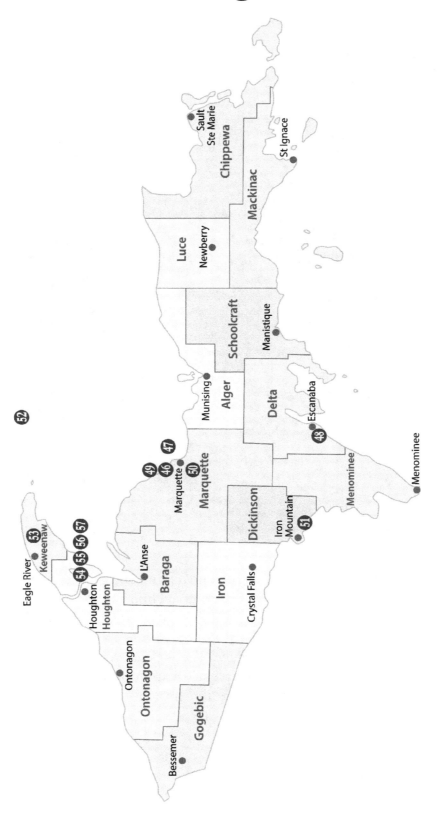

Sault
Ste Marie

Chippewa

St Ignace

Mackinac

Luce
Newberry

Schoolcraft

Manistique

Munising

Alger

Delta

Escanaba

52

47

49 46 50

Marquette

Marquette

Menominee

Menominee

Dickinson

Iron
Mountain

51

53

Keweenaw

57

56

L'Anse

Baraga

Iron

Crystal Falls

Eagle River

54 55

Houghton

Houghton

Ontonagon

Ontonagon

Gogebic

Bessemer

46 **Jackson Iron Mine Near Marquette—Negaunee**

Photograph by Brubaker *Stereoview*

The Jackson Mine was the first commercial iron mine on the Marquette iron range. The credit for finding the iron in the region has gone to Philo Everett, a geologist searching for iron deposits rumored to be in the area. Unable to locate it, he asked for the help of the local Native Americans, and Chief Marji Gesik led him to where an uprooted tree had exposed iron deposits to the ground surface. The Jackson Mine was dug on that spot. The iron deposits in the region proved to be plentiful and dozens of iron mines began in the area. Above, several tunnels can be seen leading into the cliff. This is the true beginning of iron in Michigan.

47 **Marquette Ore Dock with Schooners—Marquette**

Photograph by Unknown   *Stereoview*

This is an early view of the lower harbor ore dock in Marquette, from 1860-1870. The sailing ships are being loaded with iron ore from the Jackson Mine and others that developed in the early years. Railroad cars hauled the ore down to the ore dock in Marquette with the train riding on the top of the ore dock. Cars were opened up and the ore flowed down chutes that dropped down above the ship's hold and loaded it up. The chutes can be seen in the picture next to the schooners. Some of the cars on top can be seen as well.

48 Unloading Iron Ore—Escanaba

Photograph by F. J. Portlance   *Postcard*

This is a close-up of the upper part of an ore dock where the unloading takes place. Because of the elevation of the ore dock structure, this part of the operation is rarely seen. The dock workers are in position on top of the railroad cars to release the ore into the chutes. This method is still used today to load the modern ships. Nothing has changed because, maybe, some things simply can't be improved upon.

㊾ Among the Iron Mines—Ishpeming

Photograph by C. B. Brubaker   *Stereoview*

This picture I am sure was taken well before there were OSHA rules for safety. These three miners are drilling holes to set dynamite to break up the iron ore into manageable sizes. One man holds the long chisel while two others slam on the head of it with sledge hammers. For the record, I personally would never be the guy holding the chisel. One miss by those hammers and you are maimed for life. The more I've looked at this picture, the less I see an upside to it. This is certainly the proverbial "accident waiting to happen."

50 **Portrait of a Mining Family—Ishpeming**

Photograph by N. M. Nelson   *Cabinet Card*

This studio picture, taken in the 1880s, shows a typical mining family from the Ishpeming/Negaunee area. Their name is unknown. It appears that mom has the kids dressed up in their best clothes, but it seems that dad has just returned from work or is on his way. He's wearing work clothes in contrast to the rest of the family. Mining was a tough and dangerous job, but it provided a solid living for the families. With four offspring, this family seems to be flourishing.

🗗 **The Cornish Pump—Iron Mountain**

Photograph by L. L. Cook   *Postcard*

This contraption is known as the Cornish pump. It sits in Iron Mountain and is today surrounded by a building, which houses the Cornish Pump Museum. The pump is huge, its size not well represented in the image. It was essential to the success of iron mining in Iron Mountain. The Cornish pumping engine kept water out of Iron Mountain's richest ore-bearing mine, the Chapin, which was built over a cedar swamp. To keep the mines dry, the mine owners commissioned the Allis Company from Wisconsin to build a water pump similar to those used in Cornwall, England to keep to mines dry. The finished product was 54 feet high and weighed over 700 tons. As I said, the picture is deceptive. This beast kept three mines dry and could pump over 5 million gallons of water a day.

52 Taking the First Steps at Copper Mining—Isle Royale

Photograph by Unknown   *Cabinet Card*

Isle Royale, the Keweenaw Peninsula, and the Ontonagon region, all contained large quantities of copper, so large that the legends of the Copper Country began. Great individual pieces of copper were unearthed that weighed several tons each. Native Americans had mined for countless years, producing hundreds of prehistoric mining pits across the region. Many of the commercial mines were constructed on the tops of these ancient mines. The picture above shows the beginnings of a copper mine. Somewhere on Isle Royale, an immense section of a hill has been removed in a search for ore. If you look closely, men can be seen halfway up the cliff, sitting where they are searching for signs of ore.

53   Man and Woman with Smelter—Keweenaw Peninsula

Photograph by Unknown   *Cabinet Card*

This picture hails from the Copper Country. Some of this old equipment is a mystery to me. This is from an early copper mining operation and I believe the man is standing next to a portable smelter. The couple looks like they dressed up a bit for their photo. This would have been a very small operation from the early days, 1860-1870. At this time, a copper rush was on, wilder than the gold rush of California and a few years earlier. The copper boom began in the 1840s and the California Gold Rush was 1869. More millionaires were made in the Upper Peninsula than in the west.

🍪 **Five Million Pounds of Copper Ready for Shipment—Houghton**

Five Million Pounds of Copper Ready for Shipment, Houghton, Mich.

Photograph by E. G. Kropp   *Postcard*

Tons of smelted copper for shipping waited on the docks at Houghton and other places across the Keweenaw Peninsula. Scenes like this were repeated in locations like Hancock, Lake Linden, and Dollar Bay. The amount of copper that came from the Keweenaw region is staggering. It is estimated at 12 billion pounds! Every town north of Houghton, Michigan had a copper mine working the area. Calumet/Laurium, twin cities, became one of the wealthiest communities in Michigan and was at one time the largest city in the U.P. Now it is but a shell of itself. Most of the copper towns are now ghost towns producing no copper.

In the background can be seen the Houghton/Hancock swing bridge. The center of the bridge was on a giant gear that could swing the bridge parallel to the canal so ships could pass through then rotate back into place for railroad passage.

55 The Man Car—Hancock

Hancock, Michigan.,
...ncy Mine–Man Cage.

Photograph by Hugh C. Leighton   *Postcard*

This is a personal favorite of mine and was taken at the Quincy Mine in Hancock. It shows how the miners got down into the mine. This particular car was reputed to have dropped 5000 feet below ground, taking at least 30 people down at once. This was the core of copper mining: men and lots of them. These miners came primarily from Scandinavia, but there were also Italians, English, and Irish. The copper country was thick with people and many of them didn't get along. Old world prejudices and animosities made it hard for some to work side by side. Disputes from below ground often erupted above ground.

56 Quincy Mine Hoist Room—Hancock

Photograph by Unknown   *Cabinet Card*

Taken around 1930, this shows the hoist room at the Quincy Mine. Still standing today as a mine tour tourist attraction, the mine is a prominent landmark on the Hancock skyline. The picture shows some of the workers, but there is no identification as to their names. The Quincy Mine shut down permanently after World War II. The copper boom was long over, and the Quincy survived longer than most.

57   **Jacobsville Sandstone Quarry—Jacobsville**

Photograph by Unknown   *Cabinet Card*

I originally found this as a Copper Country photo related to copper mining. As I looked closely I realized I was looking at a rock quarry. I blew the picture up and saw streaks in the blocks they were cutting away. It was Jacobsville sandstone. Nothing looks quite like it. The white streaks on the red sandstone are quite apparent even in a black-and-white picture. Jacobsville sandstone is used in buildings in the Houghton and Calumet area. It can be found in other areas, especially in larger U.P. cities, but it was also shipped to places like Detroit and Chicago for buildings there. I've been on a shipwreck in the Straits of Mackinac that contained Jacobsville sandstone as cargo. It was headed south when a storm hit it.

Native Americans

58 **Native American Huts—Grand Island**

Photograph by Crater and Bill   *Stereoview*

This is a very rare image of the Native American settlement on Grand Island near Munising. Other than engravings, this is the only picture I've seen of this particular village. When Williams Landing was founded on Grand Island, local Natives from this village guided visitors to the island to Pictured Rocks. Munising Bay was excellent fishing for the Natives, and Grand Island provided maple sugar for the tribe, a Native American delicacy.

59 **John Boucher—Sault Ste. Marie**

AN HONEST INDIAN—OLD JOHN BOUCHER,
SAULT STE. MARIE, MICHIGAN.

Photograph by Detroit Photographic Company *Postcard*

John Boucher was a well-known Native American figure in Sault Ste. Marie. He was a jack-of-all-trades in that he held several jobs locally. He was a mail carrier who ran a dog team from the Sault to Alpena to bring mail, and was the one who brought the news of Lincoln's assassination. He was a local guide who took the more daring folks shooting the St. Mary's Rapids in his canoe. He was a friend to Michigan Governor and Sault Ste. Marie resident, Chase S. Osborn. He loved to tell stories to the early tourists of growing up as a Native, and the lore of the Ojibwa.

60 Ojibwa Medicine Lodge—Manistique

INDIAN MEDICINE LODGE

Photograph by E. C. Kropp   *Postcard*

This picture shows a traditional longhouse near Manistique and Kitch-Iti-Kipi, known as Big Springs. The longhouse was used for gatherings of different kinds: council meetings, religious ceremonies, and Native holidays. The longhouses were built using poles with reed mats, and bark stretched across forming an outer shell. These were sturdy and warm, sheltering the occupants from almost any kind of weather.

61 **Native Woman and Tipi—Unknown**

Photograph by B. F. Childs   *Stereoview*

This is another rare picture from the 1860-1870s. A Native woman is seen standing outside of her crude home. Sheets of birch bark make up the covering that wraps around cut poles tipi style. Though we often see Upper Peninsula Ojibwa in the longhouse or wigwam style of building, many of the Natives migrated away from Lake Superior in the winter, the portable tipi style made that seasonal migration possible. Though I'm sure this was not unusual, this picture is of a tipi, rarely seen in pictures of northern tribes.

(62) Ke-ga-de-sa, Chief of the Chippewas—Keweenaw

Photograph by B. F. Childs *Stereoview*

One of the real problems with photographs of Native Americans is that they are often mislabeled. This one is no exception and the picture title above is wrong. I have seen this picture with three different names on it. It is actually believed that this is a chief named The-che-bivos (Hole in the Wind) and very little is known about him. My information says he was originally from the Keweenaw Bay area. Another copy of this same picture has him labeled as How-How-Jim, Chippewa (Big Medicine.) It seems when it came to Native Americans, getting the name right was NOT a priority. It makes it nearly impossible to identify some of these individuals.

63 Chippeway Indians fishing in Birch Bark Canoes—Sault de St. Mary's

CHIPPEWAY INDIANS FISHING IN BIRCH-BARK CANOES, SAULT DE ST. MARY'S, LAKE SUPERIOR. *(After Catlin).*

Engraving by Caitlin   *Engraving*

I wanted to include this old engraving as it is one of the nicest examples showing the Ojibway fishing at the Rapids of the St. Mary's. I expect that this scene was captured near what is today Rotary Park, near where the original Methodist Mission was. The nets and canoes depict a traditional fishing expedition for the area Natives. This is one of the earliest images we have of the Soo Ojibwa.

64 Indian Village at St. Mary's River—Sault Ste. Marie

Photograph by B. F. Childs   *Stereoview*

The Native American settlement at Sault Ste. Marie is ancient. One of the few permanent settlements near Lake Superior, the rapids in the river flow fast enough that it rarely frozen in the winter, allowing year-around access to water and fish. The Ojibwa presence in this place goes back hundreds if not thousands of years. Some Native artifacts found near Marquette go back 13,000 years. The small village in the picture is the remnants of that settlement. Nestled on the banks of the St. Mary's River, it was a welcoming place for voyageurs and many settlers. When the first Soo Locks were built in 1855, they were placed between the Native village and the newly sprouting city of Sault Ste. Marie. The village was relegated to the river and became an island across from the locks. The locks were also dug through the burial ground, a monument to which is in the Locks Park in the Sault. Eventually the village was obliterated by the addition of more locks.

(65) Ojibwa Woman with Children—Sault Ste. Marie

OJIBWAY INDIANS AT
SAULT STE. MARIE MICH.

Photograph by Unknown *Postcard*

Pictures of actual Native Americans are hard to find. Many images portray them mockingly and are racist in their content. The woman and children in this picture are unknown, but they show Native culture surfacing in the traditional child carrier during a time where it was actively being discouraged. This photo depicts a clash of cultures, the one that is centuries ingrained and the other that is imposing itself upon the other.

⑥⑥   At Chief's Island—Sault Ste. Marie

Photographed by B. F. Childs   *Stereoview*

Dubbed Chief's Island, the Native Village became an island after the locks construction at the Soo. Along with the small houses, the island had a small bay away from the river current, so they could pull their canoes up onto shore. The St. Mary's River was still widely used for fishing and the fishing nets can be seen on the bow of the canoe in the background. The man in the picture might be Jack LaPete, a guide from the Marquette area who had worked up and down the Lake Superior shoreline. He was one of the Natives who guided people into Pictured Rocks.

Recreation

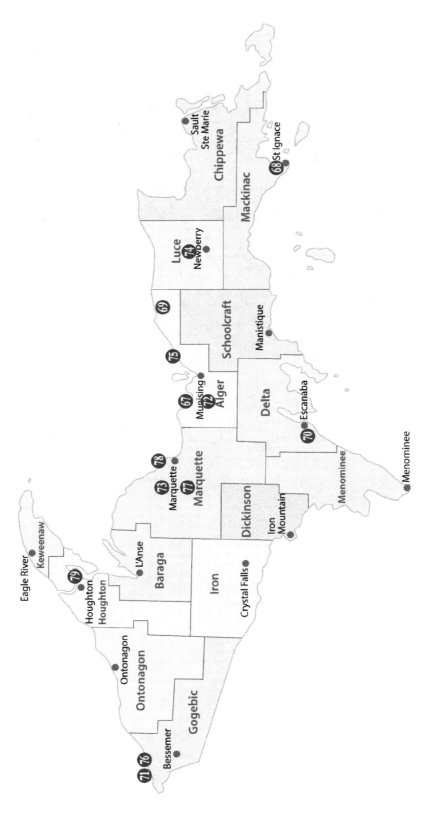

Sault
Ste Marie

Chippewa

Mackinac

68 St Ignace

Luce
74 Newberry

69

Schoolcraft

75

Manistique

61 Munising
72 Alger

Delta

Escanaba
70

Menominee

78 Marquette

73 77
Marquette Marquette

Dickinson

Menominee

Iron
Mountain

Eagle River
Keweenaw

L'Anse

Baraga

Iron

Crystal Falls

79 Houghton
Houghton

Ontonagon

Ontonagon

Gogebic

Bessemer

71 76

⑥⑦ Camp Near Au Train Lake—Au Train

Photograph by Unknown *Cabinet Card*

This picture is a favorite of mine. Au Train has always been a place where people came to relax. With resorts that began in the late 1800s, hunting and fishing has been popular here. The surrounding area teems with lakes and rivers, providing an ideal environment for all types of game and fish. Though there are no dead animals on display in this picture, the tools of the trade certainly are. One man is holding a shotgun and a fishing creel, and a net is seen slung over a tent pole. The photographer did an excellent job of capturing an iconic moment in time.

⑥⑧ **Early Castle Rock—St. Ignace**

Photograph by Unknown   *Postcard*

Still recognizable today, this picture of Castle Rock was been taken around 1930. A climb to the top provides views of the Straits, Mackinac Island and St. Ignace. A message on the back could have been written yesterday. "Arrived in St. Ignace on the 1ˢᵗ. Came by D&C Steamer and had a most enjoyable trip. We all motored to the Sault Ste. Marie and saw the Soo Locks, quite a sight to A.J. and me. This northern region is woodsy, watery, wild and wooly. We saw a porcupine cross the highway & they say deer and bear are occasionally seen near town. Hope you both are well and having a big time in Ohio. A.J. & Howard." While so many things change in the world, some seem to go on generation after generation.

69 Fishing a Beaver Dam on the Hurricane Creek—Grand Marais

31 View of Beavers' Dam on Hurricane Creek 500 ft. long and 5 ft. high, Grand Marais, Mich.

Photograph by J. V. Kinsey   *Postcard*

I've spent many years fishing beaver ponds like this. This one is on the backwaters of the Hurricane Creek, which is west of Grand Marais near the Au Sable Point Lighthouse. Upstream can be found a series of beaver ponds, which have been around since 1908, the date on the postcard. Beaver ponds are a source of some of the best trout fishing there is. The fisherman in the picture is standing on a large beaver dam. These can get quite deep depending on how long they've been there. The size of this dam makes it appear old. I'm a little bit jealous of his fancy bowler hat.

70 Out for a Sunday Drive—Escanaba

Photograph by Unknown   *Postcard*

This picture is for a personalized postcard sent in 1917, taken in Escanaba. It was taken to show off their new automobile, which was a novel thing then, and it appears they bought the best one they could find. Scarves are wrapped, the top is down and a cruise along Bay de Noc is warranted. There are no names on this to identify anyone other than the person it was sent to in Detroit.

⑦ Football Player in Snow—Ironwood

Photograph by Unknown   *Cabinet Card*

This leatherhead standing in the snow seems to be set to take on all comers for the Ironwood football team. Football here was very different from modern football. It was mostly running—passes didn't come until later. The equipment was minimal and the game was rough. Health was not a consideration. Football in the Upper Peninsula was very popular and many of the towns had teams. Places like Ironwood and Ishpeming had early professional teams.

72 Women Fishing the Au Train River—Au Train

Photograph by Unknown   *Cabinet Card*

This is another picture from the Au Train area, taken at about the same time as the other one, 1900, it shows several women fishing in the Au Train River. Everyone seems to be having a great time, just relaxing and hanging in the water. The period clothes are priceless. The entire family seems to be enjoying their time at the river in the summer. I occasionally go to a spot in Au Train that looks exactly like this one.

73 Skiing Girls Portrait—Ishpeming

Photograph by N. M. Nelson   *Cabinet Card*

Skiing is ingrained deeply into the Upper Peninsula culture. Ski flying, also known as ski jumping, has been a favorite sport all across the U.P. Brought here by the Scandinavian immigrants, ski flying has had more of an impact than any other sport on local residents. This pair of girls is no exception. The "studio" picture is exceptional for the clothing and equipment the girls are using. Notice the single ski pole and the flattened end that is dipping into the snow. These two look like they are ready to tackle any weather. Getting to school with weather back then, according to my parents, was uphill both ways and the snow was 30 feet deep. Good luck, girls.

74 Yachting on the Tahquamenon—Newberry

Photograph by Ross Leighton   *Postcard*

For over 100 years, people have been travelling down the Tahquamenon River to see the magnificent waterfalls that grace this incredible river. The picture above shows some guys heading out for an adventure. No matter where you start from, Newberry or the river mouth near Paradise, a ride up and down the river has thrilled countless visitors. The picture was taken before 1909. A message on the back reads, "Dear Friend, I am going down the river in the morning. Write and I will get it." 11/27/09 is scrawled at the top. They were embarking on an adventure to remember, I'm sure of that.

⑦⑤　Camping at Chapel Beach 1860—Munising

Photograph by B. F. Childs   *Stereoview*

This is a picture of an early expedition into Pictured Rocks. Chapel Rock is plainly visible in the distance. A couple of boats can be very faintly seen, pulled up on the shoreline. Their equipment is heavy and bulky, unlike today's ultra-light gear. The heavy wooden box their cookware is packed in would have weighed a lot and would have to be struggled through the sand to set up camp. The spectacular nature of the Pictured Rocks cliffs have amazed everyone who has seen them. Commented on in every journal going back to the voyageurs, people have been coming to view them since they were discovered.

76 **Portrait Unknown Hunter—Ironwood**

Photograph by Jacob Olli *Cabinet Card*

Talk about dressed to kill. This unknown Ironwood man is all decked out to go hunting birds in this "studio" photo. A lot of things are wrong with this picture. The clothes are obviously very new, but he is carrying a Winchester repeater for a gun. It's something someone would never use for birds. The bird carrybag around his shoulder looks ill-fitting and the subject doesn't look comfortable with any of it. It's an image that doesn't seem to suit the man.

⑦ Going to Ski at Suicide Hill—Ishpeming

Photograph by Unknown   *Cabinet Card*

It took me a while to figure out what I was looking at in this picture, which originated in a collection from Ishpeming. At first I thought it was a just a guy with skis, until more of the detail in the image became clearer. This is an event at Ishpeming's Suicide Hill, the ski flying hill. There are dozens of spectators and contestants waiting for the next jump. Look closely, and people can be seen in the trees watching from the higher vantage point. Besides Suicide Hill, there are two other ski jumping ramps: Copper Peak near Bessemer and Pine Mountain in Iron Mountain. All three places still hold competitions and the Ski Flying Hall of Fame is in Ishpeming.

⑱ Hunting Camp at Partridge Island—Marquette

Photograph by Unknown   *Cabinet Card*

Hunting camp is a cultural thing here in the U.P. First day of deer season is a paid holiday for workers, and children are excused from school, all to attend hunting camp. The camp above is from 140 years ago. The fall hunting ritual has spanned the years and traditions. Go onward. On close look, this picture has all ages of family in it and more than one family is present. No weapons are visible, but the photo is marked "Partridge Island hunting camp."

79 Working on the Aim—Hancock

Photograph by Unknown   *Cabinet Card*

This Upper Peninsula version of Annie Oakley looks like she's taking her shooting seriously. Her name is Ethel Martin, and she is apparently shooting over the Hancock Canal as it is written on the card. Her dress is typical outdoors wear for women and the hat really tops it off. Overall, this is one of those pictures you just don't see every day. I guess the hubby won't be taking off for hunting camp alone any more.

Ships and Shipping

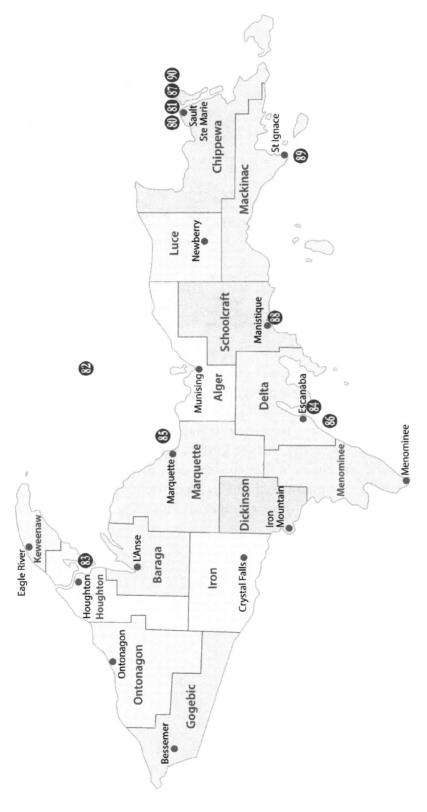

Sault
Ste Marie

Chippewa

Mackinac

St Ignace

Luce

Newberry

Schoolcraft

Manistique

Alger

Munising

Delta

Escanaba

Marquette

Marquette

Menominee

Dickinson

Iron
Mountain

Menominee

Eagle River

Keweenaw

L'Anse

Baraga

Iron

Crystal Falls

Houghton
Houghton

Ontonagon

Ontonagon

Gogebic

Bessemer

⑧⓪ **Digging the Soo Locks—Sault Ste. Marie**

Photograph by Unknown　　　　　　　　　　　　　　　　*Cabinet Card*

Everything changed when the Soo Locks opened. Before the locks, all cargo and sometimes ships would have to be portaged around the Rapids in the St. Mary's River. This was done down what is now known as Portage Ave. in Sault Ste. Marie. The picture above shows workers digging the first lock. It dates to 1854 and shows the incomplete channel. This could possibly be the earliest known photo of the locks construction. One of the things I like is the guy sitting under the tree near the top watching the construction going on below him. The completion of the locks caused an unemployment crisis in the Sault, because all those working to portage goods and ships were now out of business.

⑧ **Vessels in Transit Sault Canal—Sault Ste. Marie**

Photograph by C. B. Brubaker   *Stereoview*

The first lock after finishing. The sailing vessels are classic. One is inside the locks and another waits its turn. The copper boom had started and iron ore had just been discovered. Shipping the copper from the Keweenaw, and iron ore from Marquette, would have been next to impossible without the innovation of the locks. Soon came a free flow of immigrants and visitors as passenger ships and cruise ships began regular runs into Lake Superior establishing the region as a land of beauty and opportunity. The settling of the U.P. begins here.

82 Whaleback in Port—Unknown

Photograph by Unknown   *Cabinet Card*

There are several pictures of whalebacks in my collection, but none are as striking as this one. Most pictures of whalebacks show them mostly submerged. Whaleback ships were a unique design, adopted to ship ore across the Great Lakes and particularly Lake Superior. Their shape was designed to lessen the impact of turbulent surf. When fully loaded, they looked more like a submarine than a surface ship. Whalebacks were fairly common throughout the early 20th century. Forty-four of them were built between 1887 and 1898 mostly in Duluth, Minnesota or Superior, Wisconsin as freighters for the iron range. When loaded, whalebacks were hard to see and were often run into by ships that couldn't see them. Their hatches tended to leak and bend during stress, which made them a hazard. The whaleback is the forefather to the modern ore freighter that we commonly see now, like the Neanderthal to the modern man.

83 Loading Copper on Steamer—Houghton

Photograph by Detroit Publishing   *Postcard*

The millions of tons of copper mined in the Keweenaw had to be shipped, and every available ship was used in some capacity. In the picture, the ship being loaded is a passenger ship and not a freighter or cargo ship. A ship would rather make some money and carry extra cargo than to run empty. Most of the cruise/passenger ships took on ore whether it was copper or iron. Often they were overloaded. If a chance storm was encountered, the extra weight could send a ship to the bottom. Many shipwreck disasters involve ships carrying too much cargo.

84 **Garden Peninsula Daily Ship—Escanaba**

Photograph by Unknown   *Cabinet Card*

This is a rare picture. The ship, I wasn't able to locate the name, ran a daily route from
Escanaba. It sailed past the Stonington peninsula and took supplies to Nahma, Garden,
Fayette, and Fairport. The ship regularly took supplies and passengers back and forth
between the towns, each of which were extremely active during their heydays. It would be
nice if the picture were a bit better quality, but we have to take what we can find. As far
as I know, this is the only copy of this and we at least have that. Local supply ships like
this one were common on the Great Lakes and many times they were the only access the
residents had to the outside world. If supplies weren't properly laid in or the ship went
down in a storm, entire communities could starve during the winter.

⑧⑤   Sailors on Shore Leave—Marquette

Photograph by Werner   *Cabinet Card*

There's nothing like getting off the ship for a while. This is the captain and a couple of crew members taking a bit of time for themselves as they relax in port. Their dress identifies them as a schooner crew, with the captain in the middle. The bottle is raspberry wine. This was taken around 1890 and is probably while the rest of the crew is unloading cargo. That was often the only time they could get away from the ship for some relaxation and travelling on solid ground.

86   S.S. German in Ice—Escanaba

Photograph by Unknown   *Cabinet Card*

Sailing on the Great Lakes is dangerous. The shipping season runs through December and into January if it is still possible. Consequently, freezing temperatures can turn the largest of ships into giant floating blocks of ice. Not only was this hard to control, the added weight was immense, but if anything had to be done on deck, dealing with not slipping overboard on the ice would be hard indeed. This is a ship called the *S.S. German*. The picture was taken just as they were docking. Had they been out much longer, they might not have docked at all.

87 A Lock Full of Schooners—Sault Ste. Marie

Copyright 1905 by the Rotograph Co.
A 7556 "Full Locks", Sault Ste. Marie, Mich.

Photograph by Rotograph   *Postcard*

The Soo Locks could fit many ships in the early days as evidenced by this lock full of schooners. They are about as tight as they can be. The perspective of the picture from the top of the locks shows the decks and character of these old sailing ships. Until the construction of the steel freighters, these schooners were used for that purpose. Many of them were towed like barges with a lead ship. This schooner group is probably all together heading for a smelting plant of some kind.

88 Wreck of Car Ferry No. 4—Manistique

Photograph by Manistique Pioneer Tribune   *Postcard*

Car ferries were common in the U.P., and several are running to this day. This one, however, suffered from a simple miscalculation. The cars we are referring to here are train cars. Ferries loaded up with train cars of iron ore and took them to the Lower Peninsula, and then shipped onward by rail. As they were loading cars onto the ferry, it was overloaded on one side, which caused it to list. Within 10 minutes it had flipped completely, sending cars and ore tumbling everywhere. Since the ship was in its slip in Manistique harbor being loaded, no rescue was required. The entire crew escaped without injury.

89   Icebound in the Straits—St. Ignace

Photograph by U.S. Coast Guard   *Press Photo*

When the locks open in March, there is always a push to get the ships moving in spite of the amount of ice that still covers the Great Lakes. Often this doesn't work well, with ships getting caught in the ice, stranded on the lakes sometime for weeks. The picture above is a press photo from April 8, 1944. The caption reads: "Ice holds a freighter fleet in the Straits of Mackinac. The ships were opening the 1944 navigation system in that waterway link between Lake Michigan and Lake Huron. Ten big lake vessels are within the scope of the camera in this photograph made from a Coast Guard patrol plane." This particular year would have made this so much more important than most. It was 1944, the height of World War II. The iron ore those ships were carrying was vital to the U.S. War effort. To this day, particularly on Lake Superior, stranded freighters, racing to get to the locks, are rescued by Coast Guard ice breakers.

90 **Portrait of a Passenger Steamer in the Soo Locks—Sault Ste. Marie**

Photograph by Allan Fanjoy   *Cabinet Card*

Many of the ship photos were taken at the Soo because of their proximity to shore, so they could produce a good portrait of individual ships of the time. To this day, the locks is one of the ways to see the Great Lakes ships up close. This picture appears to have been taken from the roof of the Iroquois Hotel (Picture is earlier in the book), which was across from the lock and three stories high, giving this great perspective. The ship in the picture is a passenger steamer called the "City of Traverse." Often a ship was named after a city. Some of the details in this picture show a lot about passenger travel on the Great Lakes and the elaborate designs on the ships back then. Looking on top of the bridge, one can see a man standing next to a large carved eagle, and the open space on the bow of the ship has a large canvas draped over it for passengers to stay out of the sun.

Miscellaneous

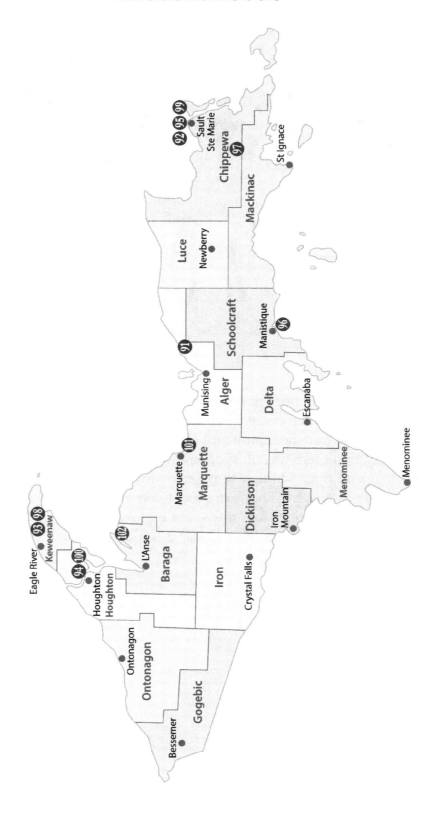

⑨ **Sled Dog Mailman—Alger County**

The Northland Express, Grand Marais, Mich.

Photograph by J. V. Kinsey   *Postcard*

Whether one believes it or not, this is how the mail was delivered for many years. Accounts of sled dog mailmen come from across the Upper Peninsula. Sled dogs were a popular winter mode of transportation and were used extensively. Looking closely at the picture, you can see that there was no specific dog breed involved. If it was big enough to pull, it could be a sled dog. Though they seem small, an individual sled dog can pull hundreds of pounds of weight. They are deceptively powerful and adapt easily to cold weather. Years ago, a cold night was measured by how many dogs one needed to sleep with to stay warm. Hence sayings like "It was a three dog night."

㉒   Bon Ton Studios—Sault Ste. Marie

Photograph by Unknown   *Cabinet Card*

It appears that this place was quite popular. Unknown to most here in the Sault, it is believed that this was a bar and boarding house, located next to the Iroquois Hotel on Portage Avenue, across from the locks. The owners were named Van Norstland and Lothian, though there are no first names available. I personally think this identification is wrong, and the photograph is of a studio with apartments above. There are many photos shot from the roof of the Iroquois Hotel that are not properly identified. Its proximity to the Iroquois makes this a good possibility.

93 **100 Year Old Store—Eagle Harbor**

THIS STORE WAS
HERE BEFORE
LINCOLN
WAS PRESIDENT

ORIGINAL
EAGLE HARBOR GENERAL STORE
OLDEST STORE IN COPPER COUNTRY
ESTABLISHED 1859
FRESH & SMOKED MEATS · GROCERIES
FROZEN FOODS · SUNDRIES
BEER · WINE TO TAKE OUT

Photograph by Unknown   *Cabinet Card*

Though this picture isn't that old, 1960s, it tells a lot about places in the U.P. This is Foley's store in Eagle Harbor. As the sign reads, it is one of the oldest buildings in Copper Country. This old store has been a staple in the Copper Country and remained open until just a few years ago. This is an awesome photo which, even though a more modern picture, still takes us back 60 years.

94 **Man with Trained Dogs—Hancock**

Photograph by P. M. Juntunen   *Cabinet Card*

I included this image because it is just plain fun. First, I have to give kudos to this guy, though there is no identification on the picture, for having these dogs so well trained. Keep in mind that there would have been a large pan flash during the photography. Most dogs would have headed for parts unknown after that.

⑨⑤   **Pulling a Railroad Engine from the Soo Canal—Sault Ste. Marie**

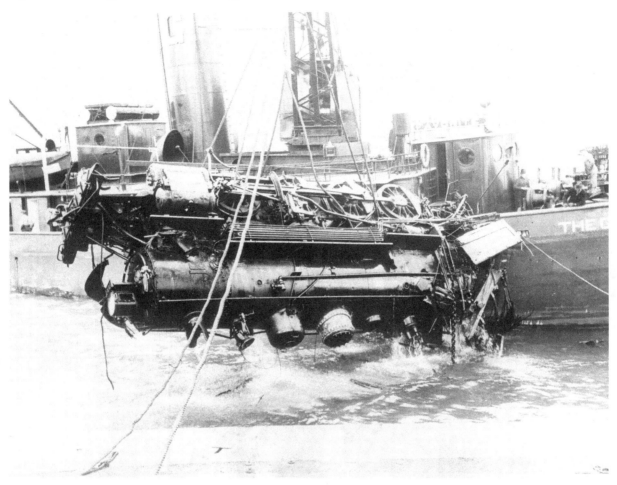

Photograph by A.P. Wire   *Press Photo*

In 1941, the railroad Bascule Bridge, which spans the St. Mary's River from Michigan to Canada, collapsed while a train was travelling across. This jackknife steel bridge can still be seen today running under the International Bridge. It jackknifed open and closed to allow ships and trains to pass through alternately. The caption on the picture reads: "Large Derrick lifting engine from canal, clearing canal so that delayed ore freighters could pass from Lake Superior through the nearby locks into the lower Great Lakes. The engine and tender has caused collapse of a railroad bridge across the canal and two trainmen were killed when the locomotive went into the canal."

96 **Getting Ready for a Sail—Manistique**

Photograph by Unknown   *Postcard*

Living on the Great Lakes provides many opportunities for getting out and enjoying whatever appeals to your fancy. This group of guys look like they are part of a sailing club, readying their boats for a day on Manistique Bay. Sailing, boating, yacht races are all a part of life on the Great Lakes. This picture was taken around 1910.

97 Wilson Passenger "Train"—Pickford

The Wilson Passenger "Train," Pickford and Sault Ste. Marie.

Photograph by Unknown

Postcard

I bet this beat the heck out of a horse and carriage. This early taxi, or "train" as it was called, ran between Sault Ste. Marie and Pickford. The picture was taken in Pickford. It is essentially a motorized surrey taking passengers back and forth to the "big city." This route to Pickford, what is today M-129, is one of the oldest highways in Michigan. It was originally part of U.S. 2 and it began in the Soo and not St. Ignace. "Ghost" U.S 2 can still be followed by going 129 to Cedarville and heading west on 134 to the Mackinac Trail. Follow it south into St. Ignace or reverse it if you want to go the other way. It was originally called the Teddy Roosevelt Highway and runs to the Pacific Ocean.

98 Store Wagon Ride—Eagle Harbor

Photograph by Unknown   *Cabinet Card*

This is a picture from Eagle Harbor in the Keweenaw and says it was taken at Foley's Store in 1904. The wagon says Foley and Smith on the side. The women make this picture what it is. They look like they are out to have a good time, probably for an event like 4th of July. They all look like they are dressed comfortably and there is a decorative shroud on the horse's flanks.

99 World War I Marching Band—Sault Ste. Marie

Photograph by Unknown   *Cabinet Photo*

This image sort of speaks for itself. The picture is labeled "Fred Rodiger World War I Band." The platform these soldiers are being towed on is a bit scary. Parades rarely move at a steady pace and I can't help thinking at some point one of these vets is going to take a tumble. Not that these tough old guys couldn't take it. It would have been fun to see these guys when they were around. There is no date for this picture so I'm figuring 1940s.

⑩ Sisters with Identical Hair—Hancock

Photograph by Haefer   *Cabinet Card*

From the late 1800s, this picture from the Copper Country really sets the period. The hair, which seems to be favored by three of the women, has never shown up in a photograph until this one. Unfortunately there is no identification on the picture so we don't know who they are. Their clothing also speaks to the period. This is a classic photo of Victorian-era women.

101   **Girl on a Harley Davidson**

The cover picture is of a young girl wishing she could go for a spin on a vintage Harley Davidson. The name on the tank is clearly visible. This is from an album of vintage photos from Ishpeming, and I expect it was taken on a farm near there. This little gem is a favorite of mine. We have all had that look on our faces the moment we sat on a motorcycle.

⑩② Journeys of a Dreamer—Lake Superior

Photograph by B. F. Childs   *Stereoview*

Taking a journey on Lake Superior is often difficult and occasionally dangerous for adventurers today. In the 1800s, it was even more so. The photograph shows photographer/explorer Brainerd. F Childs on an expedition he took along with renowned Native American guide Jack LaPete around Lake Superior to thoroughly photograph the region. Many of his photos, some of which grace this book, are some of the earliest photo images there are. The pair sailed around Lake Superior in Child's Mackinac boat named the Wanderer (pictured) to specifically photograph Ojibwa natives. He shot many other things too along the way, chronicling the settling of the Upper Peninsula. We owe a lot to those early photographer explorers.

Glossary of Terms

Cabinet Cards

These are single images mounted on a cardboard back. They vary in sizes, with the majority being 5x7, but they can get quite large. They can be displayed without a frame on a cabinet or a table. These were mostly popular in the Victorian Age and were a photographic alternative during the same time period as the stereoview.

Engravings

Engravings are some of the earliest images historians have of life before photography. As far back as the 15th century, wood-cut engravings have been the print world's pictures. These amazing pieces of artwork often were intricate images carved into wood to be used in typeset printing. Nearly every old book and publication had engraved pictures.

Lithographs

These are images created from a large, flat piece of limestone or a smooth slab of metal, inked and pressed onto high quality paper. These were difficult to make and are considered fine art prints. Lithography was originally invented in 1796 in Germany and was used primarily for sheet music and maps and evolved into pictures. Lithograph prints, highly prized for their beauty and durability, are almost always limited in number.

Postcards

Postcards, popular to this day, originated in Germany in 1865 and slowly gained ground from there, especially after 1900. Usually depicting "tourist" oriented sites, they eventually evolved into depictions of most things, including scenic sites, current events, cities and businesses. Because of the longevity of the popularity of the postcard, it is possible to view a progression through history from most places.

Photo Print

In 1881, George Eastman invented the roll film camera. Before this, film negatives were big and bulky, created from glass plates that had to be inserted into large, cumbersome cameras for every shot. Roll film allowed a camera to take more than one photograph at a time, pull out the roll, develop it and then print pictures on specialized paper. Photo prints still exist today, but the cameras are digital, requiring no film at all.

Press Release Photo

These are photo prints, usually 8x10, that are sent out as press releases to newspapers and other periodicals. Created by wire services, like United Press International (UPI) and Associated Press (AP), they depict some kind of current event, have photo identification - usually in the form of a caption. They are dated, as well.

Bellows cameras were invented in the 1850s

Stereoview (or Stereoscope)

A stereoview, popular in the mid to late 1800's, was a 4x7 card that featured two identical pictures, side by side. The images had a square shape, and some had a tombstone shape to them. When looked at through a viewer, the image was 3d. The stereoview card phased out in the early 1900s, but, for those of us old enough to remember, the tradition was revived in the 1970s with the GAF View-Master™ and View-Master reel. One of the nice things about a stereoview was that there were two choices of the same picture for preservation.

A lithograph print of a Victoria-era Stereoscope

GAF View-Master™ circa 1970

About Mikel B. Classen

Mikel B. Classen has been writing and photographing northern Michigan in newspapers and magazines for over thirty-five years, creating feature articles about the life and culture of Michigan's north country. A journalist, historian, photographer and author with a fascination for the world around him, he enjoys researching and writing about lost stories from the past. Currently he is managing editor of the *U.P. Reader* and is a member of the Board of Directors for the Upper Peninsula Publishers and Authors Association. In 2020, Mikel won the Historical Society of Michigan's George Follo Award for Upper Peninsula History. He has just released a new book, *True Tales: The Forgotten History of Michigan's Upper Peninsula* in 2022.

Classen makes his home in the oldest city in Michigan, historic Sault Ste. Marie. He is also a collector of out-of-print history books, and historical photographs and prints of Upper Michigan. At Northern Michigan University, he studied English, history, journalism and photography.

His book, *Au Sable Point Lighthouse, Beacon on Lake Superior's Shipwreck Coast* was published in 2014 and his book, *Teddy Roosevelt and the Marquette Libel Trial* was published in 2015, both by the History Press. He has a book of fiction called *Lake Superior Tales*, published by Modern History Press, which won the 2020 U.P. Notable Book Award. His book, *Points North,* is a non-fiction travel book published in 2019 by Modern History Press. It has received the Historical Society of Michigan's "Outstanding Michigan History Publication," along with the 2021 U.P. Notable Book Award.

To learn more about Mikel B. Classen and to see more of his work, go to his website at www.mikelbclassen.com.

Index

What Were Pioneer Days *Really* Like in the U.P.?

The combination of mining, maritime and lumbering history created a culture in the U.P. that is unique to the Midwest. Discover true stories of the rough and dangerous times of the Upper Peninsula frontier that are as enjoyable as they are educational. You'll find no conventional romantic or whitewashed history here. Instead, you will be astonished by the true hardships and facets of trying to settle a frontier sandwiched among the three Great Lakes.

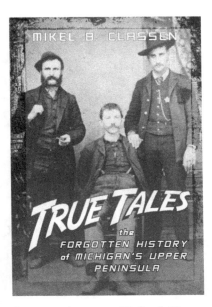

These pages are populated by Native Americans and the European immigrants, looking for their personal promised land-whether to raise families, avoid the law, start a new life or just get rich... no matter what it took. Mineral hunters, outlaws, men of honor creating civilization out of wilderness and the women of strength that accompanied them, the Upper Peninsula called to all. Among the eye-opening stories, you'll find *True Tales* includes:

- Dan Seavey, the infamous pirate based out of Escanaba
- Angelique Mott, who was marooned with her husband on Isle Royale for 9 months with just a handful of provisions and no weapons or tools
- Vigilantes who broke up the notorious sex trafficking rings--protected by stockades, gunmen, and feral dogs--in Seney, Sac Bay, Ewen, Trout Creek, Ontonagon and Bruce Crossing
- Klaus L. Hamringa, the lightkeeper hero who received a commendation of valor for saving the crews of the Monarch and Kiowa shipwrecks
- The strange story of stagecoach robber Reimund (Black Bart) Holzhey
- The whimsical tale of how Christmas, Michigan got its moniker
- The backstories of famous pioneers, such as Peter White, George Shiras III, Governor Chase Osborn and many others

"This book is a gold mine of vacation possibilities, providing dozens of fascinating little-known facts about many of the innumerable attractions found in Michigan's Upper Peninsula. While most would agree that there exists no more interesting place to explore than Michigan's U.P., the way Mikel describes the individual points of interest exponentially enhances the qualities of each attraction. With the aid of a near countless parade of carefully selected historical images, Mikel paints a picture the reader will not ever forget." -- Michael Carrier, author of *Murder on Sugar Island* (Jack Handler mysteries)

Learn more at MikelBClassen.com

From Modern History Press

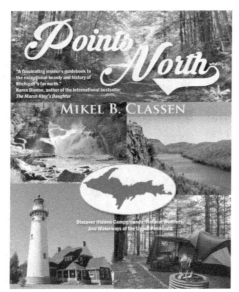

Winner of the State History Award from the Historical Society of Michigan

This book has been a labor of love that spans many years. The love is for Michigan's Upper Peninsula (U.P.), its places and people. I've spent many years exploring the wilderness of the U.P., and one thing has become apparent. No matter what part you find yourself in, fascinating sights are around every corner. There are parks, wilderness areas, and museums. There are ghost towns and places named after legends. There are trails to be walked and waterways to be paddled. In the U.P., life is meant to be lived to the fullest.

In this book, I've listed 40 destinations from every corner of the U.P. that have places of interest. Some reflect rich history, while others highlight natural wonders that abound across the peninsula. So many sights exist, in fact, that after a lifetime of exploration, I'm still discovering new and fascinating places that I've never seen or heard of. So, join in the adventures. The Upper Peninsula is an open book--the one that's in your hand.

"Without a doubt, Mikel B. Classen's book, *Points North*, needs to be in every library, gift shop and quality bookstore throughout the country--particularly those located in Michigan's Lower Peninsula. Not only does Classen bring alive the 'Hidden Campgrounds, Natural Wonders and Waterways of the Upper Peninsula' through his polished words, his masterful use of color photography make this book absolutely beautiful. *Points North* will long stand as a tremendous tribute to one of the most remarkable parts of our country."

--Michael Carrier, author *Murder on Sugar Island'*

"Mikel Classen's love for Michigan's Upper Peninsula shines from every page in Points North, a fascinating insider's guidebook to the exceptional beauty and history of Michigan's far north. Whether you're still in the planning stages of your trip, or you're looking back fondly on the memories you created-even if you wish merely to enjoy a virtual tour of the Upper Peninsula's natural wonders from the comfort of your armchair, you need this book."

--Karen Dionne, author of the international bestseller, *The Marsh King's Daughter*
Learn more at www.PointsNorthBooks.com

From Modern History Press www.ModernHistoryPress.com

Pirates, thieves, shipwrecks, sexy women, lost gold, and adventures on the Lake Superior frontier await you!

In this book, you'll sail on a ship full of gold, outwit deadly shapeshifters, battle frontier outlaws and even meet the mysterious agent that Andrew Jackson called "the meanest man" he ever knew. Packed with action, adventure, humor, and suspense, this book has something for every reader. Journey to the wilds of the Lake Superior shoreline through ten stories that span the 19th century through present day including "The Wreck of the Marie Jenny," "The Bigg Man," "Wolf Killer," and "Bullets Shine Silver in the Moonlight."

Mikel B. Classen is a longtime resident of Sault Sainte Marie in Michigan's Upper Peninsula. His intimacy of the region, the history and its culture gives this book a feel of authenticity that is rarely seen. As a writer, journalist, columnist, photographer, and editor with more than 30 years experience, his breadth of knowledge is unparalleled.

"It's clear that Mikel B. Classen knows and loves the Lake Superior area of Michigan and brings it to life in a delightful way. If you want frequent laughs, unusual characters who jump off the page, and the fruit of a highly creative mind, you've got to read this little book."

Bob Rich, author, *Looking Through Water*

"Just read Lake Superior Tales. Oh my...! My favorite chapters were: Bullets Shine in the Moonlight; The Wreck of the Marie Jenny; Wolf Killers and Cave of Gold. What a twist with Abigail being with the bad guy! It looks like you did your research and it was very well written. You kept me wanting to read more to find out what happens next."

Sharon Brunner, *U.P. Book Review*

From Modern History Press

Learn more at www.MikelBClassen.com

9 781615 997244